Rebellion's Song

Program Consultants

Stephanie Abraham Hirsh, Ph.D.
Associate Director
National Staff Development Council
Dallas, Texas

Louise Matteoni, Ph.D.
Professor of Education
Brooklyn College
City University of New York

Karen Tindel Wiggins
Social Studies Consultant
Richardson Independent School District
Richardson, Texas

Renee Levitt
Educational Consultant
Scarsdale, New York

Steck-Vaughn Company

A Subsidiary of National Education Corporation

Rebellion's Song

BY
Melissa Stone

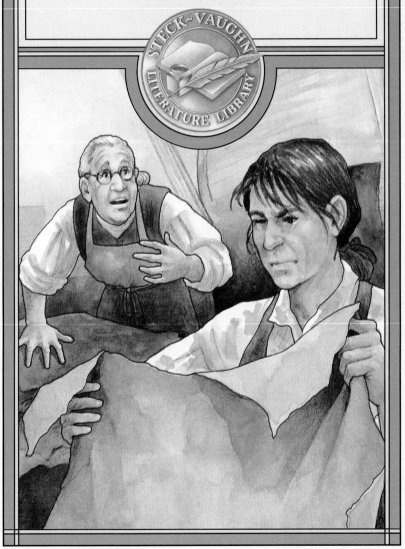

Steck-Vaughn Literature Library
Moments in American History

RISKING IT ALL
REBELLION'S SONG
CREATIVE DAYS
RACING TO THE WEST
YOU DON'T OWN ME!
CLOUDS OF WAR
A CRY FOR ACTION
LARGER THAN LIFE
FLYING HIGH
BRIGHTER TOMORROWS

Illustrations: Konrad Hack: cover art; pp. 8-9, 11, 12, 15, 16-17, 19; D.J. Simison: pp. 20-21, 22, 25, 27, 28, 31; Ron Himler: pp. 32-33, 34, 37, 38, 41, 43; Lyle Miller: pp. 44-45, 47, 49, 50-51, 53, 55; Christa Kieffer: pp. 56-57, 58, 61, 62-63, 64, 67; Melinda Bordelon: pp. 68-69, 70-71, 73, 75, 76, 79.

Project Editor: Anne Souby

Design: Kirchoff/Wohlberg, Inc.

CONTENTS

PHILLIS WHEATLEY ➤
A new America, just waking
to its greatness, produces its
first black poet.

ABIGAIL ADAMS ➤
She wanted women to
participate fully in the
birth of a new country.

◀**WILLIAM BILLINGS**
He wrote songs that
stirred the hearts of
Revolutionary soldiers.

1780

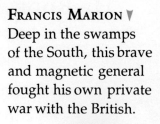

FRANCIS MARION ▼
Deep in the swamps
of the South, this brave
and magnetic general
fought his own private
war with the British.

PAUL REVERE ▲
His midnight ride lives
forever in the hearts
of Americans.

NATHAN HALE ➤
A young schoolteacher
gave his life in an
attempt to help his
country live.

7

PAUL REVERE
HE RODE AT MIDNIGHT

The tension in Boston is mounting every day. The redcoats are on every street corner. They march and drill throughout the day.

All we want is for them to go back to England. They're strangers to us now. We no longer feel like Englishmen. This is a new land — our land. It has nothing to do with the British!

I don't know, but I feel that something is going to happen soon!

PAUL Revere tossed and turned in his bed. He could not get the faces of the ever-present British soldiers out of his mind.

Finally, at 6:00 A.M., he woke his wife. "Rachel, I'm troubled. I haven't slept all night. I must make a decision, and I don't know what to do. Boston is our home. Yet the British are bleeding us to death in order to raise money to keep their soldiers here. Every day there is a new tax."

"But, Paul," said Rachel, "they say they are doing this to protect us. We have no army of our own."

"Protect us? Why? We can take care of ourselves. We can make our own laws and collect our own taxes." He paused.

"We are no longer British. We have our own way of living." Even as he spoke, Paul Revere knew what he must do.

"People may call me a rebel or a troublemaker," he said, "but I am going to fight British rule any way I can. One of our leaders, Samuel Adams, has asked me to join his secret group of rebels. They call themselves the Sons of Liberty."

Rachel reached for his hand in the soft morning light. She loved her husband. He did not have the money or the education that some had. But he had strength and determination and courage.

A few weeks later, Revere's son ran into their little home on North Square and cried: "Father! Come! There's trouble on King Street!" Revere grabbed a coat and followed his son into the street. What he saw made his heart beat faster.

On one side of the street were his friends and neighbors. On the other side was a lone British guard. The townspeople were taunting the young man. In his bright red coat he stood for all that they hated.

"Watch this one! Right in the middle of the red jacket!" said a boy. He threw an icy snowball at the guard and struck him hard in the chest. Others joined in the shouting. The crowd grew larger, the noise louder. More people picked up snow and rolled it into tight snowballs. "Lobster-backs! Redcoats! Go home!" they shouted.

The British guard looked around anxiously and called to other guards for help. This hostile crowd was more than he could handle. More British regulars came running, with rifles loaded.

"Don't fire," called their captain, "but stand firm." The redcoats stood with rifles at attention.

The unarmed townspeople faced a wall of soldiers with loaded rifles. It seemed so unfair that they grew even angrier. A few rushed toward one of the guards, fists ready.

Revere could scarcely believe what happened after that. He heard someone shout, "Fire!" And suddenly flames leaped from the British guns.

The people gasped, then cried out with pain and disbelief. How could something like this happen in Boston? The crowd ran wildly in all directions, searching for cover.

Three men lay dead and eight wounded. The British soldiers turned and marched away as the blood of the victims changed the white snow to crimson. As their footsteps died away, the sobbing of the survivors filled the night.

"It was a massacre, nothing less than a massacre," said Paul Revere later. "We cannot stand idly by any longer. It is one thing to occupy our homes and tax us into poverty. Now they intend to kill our people. We must strike back." So that people would never forget what happened that snowy night in March of 1770, Revere engraved a printing plate showing the British soldiers firing on the defenseless townspeople. "Let this horrible deed be recorded in history forever," he said.

B Y 1775, many colonists shared Revere's anger. The time had come to break away from Britain. But that meant having a war. Grimly, both sides prepared for the worst.

Colonists formed groups called Minutemen. The name meant just that: they would be ready in a minute to go to battle for freedom. Britain sent extra troops to Boston, 5,000 fighting men in all.

Rumors spread that the leaders of the Sons of Liberty would be jailed. So, on April 15, Sam Adams and John Hancock, two of the most important rebel leaders, decided to slip out of the city to avoid arrest.

Before leaving, they met secretly with Paul Revere. "Paul," said Adams, "we have to go to Lexington for a while. The Reverend Jonas Clark has offered to let us stay with him."

"Tell me what I can do to help," Revere said.

Adams dropped his voice to a whisper. "Nothing yet," he said. "But beware: the British may decide to march to Concord. They know that's where our gunpowder and rifles are stored. If they destroy our weapons, they'll break the back of the rebellion. You *must* warn us as soon as you know anything."

Again Revere nodded. He felt honored, but also a little frightened. What if something went wrong? What if the British captured him? What if he couldn't get the message through in time?

"Remember, Paul," said Hancock, "we're counting on you."

Revere pushed his doubts aside. "I won't let you down," he promised. "My men will stand watch, and I'll get the message to you if the British try anything."

OR three days, the city remained calm. But on the night of April 18, one of the Sons of Liberty knocked on Revere's door.

"The British are gathering on the Boston Common. They're getting ready to go to Concord. It looks as if they'll be crossing the Charles River."

Revere felt his hands grow clammy and his throat turn dry. But he slipped out of his house and hurried to the Old North Church a short distance from the water's edge. Its high tower could be seen for miles around, and the Sons of Liberty had planned to use it for a secret signal. Revere found the sexton and asked him to hang two lanterns in the belfry of the church tower.

"But why?" asked the sleepy churchman.

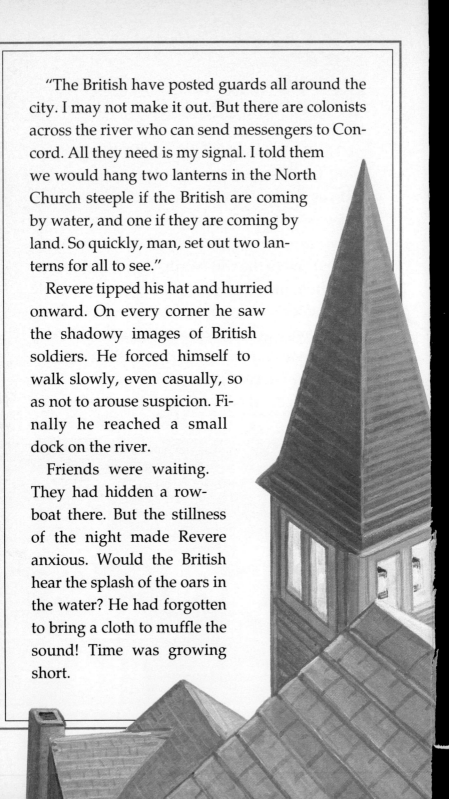

"The British have posted guards all around the city. I may not make it out. But there are colonists across the river who can send messengers to Concord. All they need is my signal. I told them we would hang two lanterns in the North Church steeple if the British are coming by water, and one if they are coming by land. So quickly, man, set out two lanterns for all to see."

Revere tipped his hat and hurried onward. On every corner he saw the shadowy images of British soldiers. He forced himself to walk slowly, even casually, so as not to arouse suspicion. Finally he reached a small dock on the river.

Friends were waiting. They had hidden a rowboat there. But the stillness of the night made Revere anxious. Would the British hear the splash of the oars in the water? He had forgotten to bring a cloth to muffle the sound! Time was growing short.

"Paul," whispered his friend, "Mistress Reynolds lives up the road. I'll run to her house and get something to muffle the sounds of the oars."

In no time at all his friend was back. "There was no time to look about. Mistress Reynolds tore off her petticoat for us to use. Here, Paul, wrap it around the oars."

AS he rowed silently and smoothly across the river, Revere saw a British transport ship looming ahead. The bright moonlight lit up the ship as well as his own rowboat. Holding his breath, Revere prayed that none of the British soldiers would glance his way. Slowly, fearfully, he slid past the big ship.

A group of colonists embraced him as he reached the other side.

"We saw your signal in the Old North Church," said one. "And we've sent out a couple of messengers. But to be honest, I doubt they'll make it. The British have posted guards on every road leading to Concord and Lexington."

Revere grimaced. "Well," he said, "*I'm* going to make it. I'll use shortcuts that the British don't know. And somehow, I'll get the message through."

"Here's your mount," another colonist spoke up, leading a horse out of the bushes.

Revere swung up into the saddle.

"I can't make any mistakes," he thought as he grabbed the reins. "The whole countryside is counting on me. If I get out the warning, we have a chance to keep the British from destroying our supplies at Concord. Otherwise, they'll win the day."

AS Revere headed out, he trained his eyes on the narrow road ahead, looking for roadblocks. Mile after mile he flew, always at full speed, always urging the horse to gallop faster. Rounding one turn in the road, he suddenly saw two British officers on horseback. They spotted him, but he quickly veered off the road, forcing his horse through thick forests and over stone walls. Soon he had outdistanced them.

When he reached the town of Medford, he dashed through the streets, shouting: "Sound the alarm! The British are coming! The British are coming! Get your gun, powder, and shot." Then he set forward to Lexington.

Because of his warning cries, the Minutemen were awakened and prepared. They gathered on the green at Lexington, their muskets loaded. Dawn came. It was April 19, 1775. In the distance the approaching drums of the British could be heard. The sounds of marching feet, 1,000 strong, broke through the morning stillness. The Americans waited. The first battle between the British and the Americans would begin in a few short minutes.

The American Revolution had indeed begun!

WILLIAM BILLINGS
THE MUSIC OF INDEPENDENCE

You and I are tanners. We work with animal skins. I trained you well and you are good at your trade. So why do you daydream of becoming a musician? You have no schooling as a composer. You have no voice. In fact, some people say they cannot stand listening to you!

Don't make a fool of yourself. Give up your dream! I beg you to concentrate on your trade! You will never be a musician!

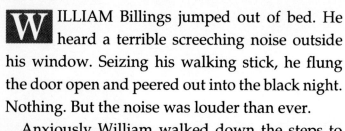

WILLIAM Billings jumped out of bed. He heard a terrible screeching noise outside his window. Seizing his walking stick, he flung the door open and peered out into the black night. Nothing. But the noise was louder than ever.

Anxiously William walked down the steps to his front gate. He looked at the signpost he had recently put up. It read, "Billings—Music." As he approached the sign, he heard loud wailing cries. The wails grew into shrieks that split the night air. William thought a wild animal might be attacking some poor creature. Then he saw the shadowy figures of two neighborhood children crouching under his sign.

"Hey there!" he called nervously. "What is the matter?"

As soon as he spoke, the children jumped up and ran off, laughing and giggling as they went.

William shook his head in anger and relief. He didn't like their pranks, but he was glad there was no real trouble. He glanced around to see if anyone else had noticed the disturbance.

Just then William spotted a note pinned to the top of his sign. He pulled it down and opened it. It read: "Our screams may sound awful. But they're better than the music you make!"

A feeling of despair flooded over William. He tore the note to shreds. Then he hurried back inside his house.

"Why do they treat me this way?" he asked his wife Mary the next morning. "Why do they always make fun of me?"

Mary handed him a cup of tea. "Well, perhaps they simply don't like your music," she suggested. Then she added, "Or perhaps they laugh at you because you are different. Perhaps you make them feel uncomfortable."

"You mean, because of the way I look?" William's voice was filled with bitterness. He was sensitive about his disabilities. He had been born blind in one eye. He walked with a limp because one leg was shorter than the other. One of his arms was small and weak. He had a coarse, rasping voice that sounded like chalk squeaking on a chalkboard.

"Well, it's not just your body. It's everything—your clothes, your hair, everything. Look at yourself in a mirror, William." Mary wasted no words. She always said exactly what she thought.

William glanced down at himself. He saw his old, ragged shirt. It was covered with stains from working with animal skins. His trousers, too, were old and grimy. Then he ran his fingers through his hair. It was thick and matted and came down over his eyes.

"Face it, William. You don't keep yourself very tidy."

Suddenly William slammed his fist down on the table.

"I am an artist!" he cried. "Don't you understand? I can't be bothered with powdered wigs and perfumes! I am a musician! A composer!"

"No, William," Mary said evenly. "You are a tanner. You make leather. Music may be your hobby, but you've never made any money with it. You earn your money as a tanner."

WILLIAM was too angry to respond. He stormed out the front door and went directly to the tannery. It was true, he told himself. He was nothing but a tanner. He had been working at the tannery since 1760, nine long years ago. He hated the greasy feel of wet animal skins. The strong smell of drying leather made him dizzy. But he kept this job because it paid well. Today, however, he was not in a mood to think about money.

"Mr. Johnson!" he shouted as he opened the door to the tannery.

"William!" Mr. Johnson shouted back, coming from behind a stack of skins. Holding out a piece of leather covered with chalk marks, he shouted: "How many times have I told you not to write your songs on my leather! You ruin it!"

"Well," William replied hotly, "you won't have to worry about that anymore. I am leaving your tannery. I'll work here no longer. And I'll write my songs elsewhere from now on!"

"What?" Mr. Johnson wiped his hands on his apron and moved out to face William.

"Did I hear you correctly?"

"I told you. I am leaving."

"But why? What are you going to do?"

"I am going to work full-time on my music. I will compose songs. I'm going to give music lessons and sell copies of my songs. I'm a musician, not a tanner!"

"You can't be serious," Mr. Johnson said, starting to smile.

"What makes you think I'm not serious?" William said angrily.

"Well, do not take offense, William," Mr. Johnson said as his grin grew wider, "but I've heard some of your music …"

William did not wait to hear the rest of the sentence. He stomped out of the tannery.

FOR the rest of the day, he put signs up around the city of Boston. "Professional musician," the signs declared. "Willing to give singing lessons. Beginners welcome." After putting up the signs, he headed for his favorite tavern and sat down next to his friend Jedd.

"I know my music is unusual," he told his friend. "But that doesn't mean it's bad. My songs are bright and strong and powerful, not like the old slow tunes that everyone sings."

Although William was confident, Jedd shook

his head. William's music did not follow the established rules of the day. Most songs people sang sounded alike. But William's music was startling; he put chords together in a way that hadn't been done before.

"Have you ever had any lessons?" Jedd asked casually.

"Just what the choirmaster taught me when I was a boy," William admitted.

"Then why do you think you're able to write music?"

"Well, I—I," William searched for the right words. "I've studied every music book I could find. I've memorized all the song books the choir uses. And I've been writing my own songs for years."

He went home to work on his music. William's wife, for one, did not find William's songs appealing. Along with many other people, she preferred the more common style.

"Frankly," she grumbled to her friends, "I would rather listen to him snore than sing!"

IN the first weeks after William quit his job, the Billings family used up all their savings. William's music business brought in little money. Day after day he waited for pupils to come to him. A few did trickle in, but not enough to support his family. William didn't seem to notice. He thought only of his own music and welcomed the chance to pursue it.

"For the first time in my life I feel truly free," he told his wife. "This is my time to write the music that is singing in my head."

As he labored over his new songs, he forgot his troubles. He felt full of creative ideas. Songs seemed to pour out of him. For William, this was a time of pure happiness.

And soon, choirs all over Boston began singing his songs. As his songs became popular, William was accepted as a teacher of music. He showed singers how to use a pitch pipe and a cello to establish and maintain pitch. Never before had people used any musical instruments to help their singing.

William's wife was still a skeptic. "I'm glad you're following your interests, William," she said, "but how will we manage? How do you plan to support your family? We are running out of everything—bread, meat, salt, kerosene. And winter is coming. The children need clothes. How can I buy cloth to make clothes when I have no money?"

"You worry too much," William replied. "We'll get by. We may have to do with old clothes, but Providence will see us through. The things of this world are with us a short time. My music will last forever!"

By the year 1770, William had completed 125 songs. He took them to a printer to be published. He called his book *The New England Psalm Singer*.

BUT, the nation was stirring restlessly. Many people wanted independence from England. Rebel leaders in Boston were calling for a revolution. William's music seemed to match America's growing spirit of rebellion. It was strong and loud and free-flowing. More and more people began to appreciate it. They were looking for something different from the old songs—they were looking for something with a true American flavor.

"This is quite a book," said the printer.

"Yes," chimed in his assistant. "Your lively songs really stir the spirit."

The printer wanted a special title page for the book, so he asked William's friend, Paul Revere, to design it. William was very excited about his book's success. He devoted himself to learning even more about new forms of music.

He also became an enthusiastic supporter of the move toward independence. Soon after the first battle of the war, William began adapting some of his psalm tunes. He wrote new words and changed them into war songs. "Chester" became a favorite. It was a rousing song that encouraged the colonists to be fearless and throw off the chains of England. These songs became America's first popular music.

One day William sat at his table. Sighing, he

looked at the bills spread in front of him. Once again he would have to ask the shopkeepers for more time. He was never going to make money. He would probably die a poor man. His family would always need more than he could give. Sadness filled his spirit.

A faraway sound interrupted his thoughts. He cocked his head.

Through the open window came the sound of troops marching toward the battlelines. Music floated above the rhythm of marching feet. What was that melody? As the sound came closer, William jumped up. The soldiers were marching to his song! It was "Chester," and the troops were singing it to keep their spirits up as they marched to war.

William smiled to himself. His music had found its place at last.

Nathan Hale

A Spy for His Country

"Colonel Knowlton, one of the things I find hardest about being a general is asking someone to do something that I wouldn't want to do myself. After all, who wants to be a spy? Think of the risk … and the penalty if you're caught! And the loss of honor…. But we've got to find out what the British are planning. Everything depends on it."

"Yes, sir, General Washington! We'll get someone behind their lines to find out!"

M EN," said Lieutenant Colonel Thomas Knowlton, "I need your help." His voice was tense. He glanced around the circle of officers. In the fading light, he could barely see their faces.

But that didn't matter; he knew who each one was. He had hand-picked all 120 of them. For several weeks, these men had been training in Connecticut. They were getting ready to fight the British. Colonel Knowlton knew his officers were strong, loyal, and brave. But now, on September 8, 1776, he needed something more. He needed a man with a special kind of courage and daring. He needed a spy!

"As you know," he said, "the British are moving through Long Island. They will probably try to attack New York City soon."

"We'll stop 'em, sir!" piped up one of the men.

Colonel Knowlton smiled grimly. "Well, son, we can't stop them if we don't know which way they're coming. Right now we don't know when or how they'll make their move. We don't even know for sure how many troops they have. That's why General George Washington has asked me to find a volunteer. We need someone to slip behind enemy lines and gather information."

Everyone grew silent. One by one, the men looked away from their leader. They knew that to slip behind enemy lines was to become a spy. No one wanted to go on a spy mission. A spy had to work all alone, surrounded by enemies, with no help from anyone.

"Well?" asked Colonel Knowlton gruffly. "Who will volunteer?"

Still the men remained silent.

The Colonel turned to George Dudley. George was one of the most experienced soldiers in the unit.

"How about you, Dudley?" Colonel Knowlton asked.

George spoke up quickly. He said, "Sir, I am willing to fight the British. I am willing to fight anytime, anywhere. But I will not creep about like a rat or a weasel! If I die in this war, I want to die with honor. I don't want to be hanged in disgrace." George Dudley knew how people felt about spies. No one trusted them. No one would speak freely before them. Spies were avoided by their fellow countrymen.

The other men in the circle nodded their agreement. To them, spying was dirty, underhanded work.

Just then one of the younger officers spoke up. "I will do it!"

All eyes turned toward the 21-year-old captain, Nathan Hale. Before the war, Nathan had attended Yale University. Then he had become a schoolteacher. He was a thoughtful and honest young man and didn't know a thing about spying. He seemed to be the least likely candidate.

"I'll do it, Colonel," Nathan repeated. "I know nothing about spying, but I'll learn. I wish to be useful. If General Washington needs a spy, then I'll be one."

Colonel Knowlton nodded, gratefully accepting Nathan's offer.

Unfortunately, Colonel Knowlton didn't have much to teach Nathan about spying. The colonel was a superb commander, but he had no experience in this kind of work. He knew nothing about safety measures for spies.

"Just go to Long Island and find out what's going on," he said. "Take good notes. And try to come back alive." But he did not give Nathan any secret code to use or a secret way of sending messages to him. The colonel didn't even consider issuing false papers to explain why Nathan was leaving the unit.

WITHIN a couple of days, Nathan was packed and ready to leave the training camp. His friend, William Hull, stopped him at the gate.

"Nathan," said William, "I will be honest with you. I don't think you should go on this mission. It's dangerous. And you have no real protection!"

"Don't worry, William," said Nathan, patting his friend's shoulder. "I'll be careful."

"But if you do come back alive, what about your honor? Spying is so—so—dishonest. No one will ever trust you again. After all, who can trust a spy?"

"I'm sorry you feel that way," Nathan said quietly. "But I disagree. I believe this mission is as honorable as any other. Right now America is fighting for her life. If we lose the war, we lose our liberty. We cannot let that happen. We must do whatever we can to win the war."

"But what about your own future?" William persisted.

"If America loses the war, I have no future."

"That may be true," William conceded. "But I still don't think you're the man for this job. You're too honest. If you were caught, I doubt if you could tell a good lie to save your life!"

"Well, William," said Nathan, "I'll face that if I have to. Let us hope I won't have to."

AFTER giving his friend a quick embrace, Nathan Hale set out to cross through the British lines. On September 12, he slipped aboard a boat headed for Long Island. He arrived there safely. Then he had to slip past the British guards in the shipyard.

"What is your purpose on this island?" a guard asked him.

Nathan paused for a minute. He knew he could not tell the truth. But he found it very difficult to lie. At last he said, "I am a schoolteacher, sir. I am here to take a new job." He felt this was a good answer. After all, he told himself, he *was* a schoolteacher. And this *was* a new job.

"Do you have any papers?" demanded the guard.

Nathan realized he had no papers, but he thought quickly.

"Just my college diploma," said Nathan, pulling his diploma from his bag.

The guard studied it a minute. Then he handed it back to Nathan.

"Go ahead," he said. "But be careful. There's a war on, you know."

"Yes, I will. Thank you, sir," said Nathan. He hurried out of the shipyard.

For the next few days, Nathan watched the British army. He studied its size and position. He took many notes about the number of men and weapons. Finally, he was ready to return to Connecticut. But the British moved too quickly for him. Before he could leave Long Island, they attacked. British General William Howe led his troops into New York City on September 15. This forced the Americans to retreat. It also made Nathan's report useless.

AT that point, Nathan could have returned to Connecticut and rejoined his unit. But he wanted to get new information that would be useful to General Washington. So he made a bold decision. He followed the British into New York City. He knew this would put him in a very dangerous situation.

When Nathan arrived, he studied the British movements. He made sketches of their positions.

He folded each slip of paper and hid it in the sole of his shoe. By September 21, he had enough information; he was ready to return to Colonel Knowlton. But as he tried to leave the city, British guards stopped him.

"Who are you? Why are you trying to leave?" demanded one guard.

"I am a schoolteacher," said Nathan. "I am on my way to see friends in Connecticut." Again he felt pleased with his answer. It wasn't exactly the truth, but it wasn't a lie, either. Nathan pulled his diploma from his bag and showed it to the guard.

The guard glanced at it, then nodded his head. Nathan was about to go through when a second guard appeared. This second guard was Samuel Hale, one of Nathan's cousins. Samuel was fighting on the British side.

"I know this man!" cried Samuel. "He is my cousin! He is in the American army!"

British guards immediately seized Nathan. They began to search him. One guard found the notes hidden in Nathan's shoe. With that evidence, they marched him off to General Howe.

"All right, soldier," said General Howe sternly. "What do we have here?"

Nathan took a deep breath. Then he confessed everything. He couldn't help it. He could not bring himself to tell a real lie.

"It is true, sir," he said proudly. "I am an American officer. I have been here in New York City on a spy mission."

General Howe remained silent a moment. Nathan's honest pride in the American cause astounded and angered him.

"I want this man hanged!" he cried. "And I want it done quickly!"

"But, sir," whispered one of the general's aides. "Shouldn't we put him on trial first?"

"Forget the trial. This is war time. I want this

man hanged tomorrow morning!" General Howe glared at Nathan for a moment. Then he turned and walked away.

THAT night Nathan sat alone in the prisoners' quarters. Calmly, politely, he asked the guards to send in a clergyman. They refused. Next he asked the guards to bring him a Bible. Again they refused. Nathan sat, waiting for the dawn.

At last, the sun rose. The time had come. Nathan's brief young life was ending. But before he was hanged, Nathan Hale spoke the words of a true patriot, words that are remembered and repeated to this very day:

"I only regret that I have but one life to lose for my country."

FRANCIS MARION
THE SWAMP FOX

I've hunted and fished in these salt marshes and swamps since I was a boy. Some people think this terrain along the coast of South Carolina is frightening. Walls of wild, tangled plants close in all around. Soft, spongy mud lies under the water that stretches on and on and on.

But I see secret trails running through the thick plant growth. I can find hard ground—even islands—in the swampy water. And from these hidden places I can hear the sounds of the enemy setting up camp.

AS Francis Marion strolled across the army base in Charleston, South Carolina, he heard someone calling his name.

"Colonel Marion! Colonel Marion!"

Marion turned and saw Captain Alexander McQueen hurrying toward him.

"Colonel Marion, a few of us are gathering for a celebration tonight. Would you join us at eight?"

Marion smiled. "Another celebration? You're always planning something. What's the occasion this time?"

Captain McQueen replied, "Well, you know how this Revolutionary War has been going. The men fight hard during the battles. They need a chance to relax and have some fun when there's a break in the fighting."

"Yes, I guess we need to take the opportunity when we have it," agreed Marion. "See you this evening."

When Marion arrived at McQueen's that night in March 1780, he found the house filled with guests. Marion made his way upstairs to the main dining room. There he saw Captain McQueen talking to one of the servants.

"Lock all the doors!" he heard him order with a merry laugh. "This celebration is going to last all night. And no one is going to leave until I say so!"

Suddenly Marion felt his muscles tighten. He did not like the idea of locked doors. Nothing made him more unhappy than the feeling of being trapped. Quietly he walked over to the second-story window. When no one was watching, he flung it open and jumped out.

As he hit the ground, Marion felt a sharp pain shoot through his ankle. He hobbled back to the army base and found the doctor. The doctor confirmed his fear. Marion had broken his ankle. The next day the army commander ordered Colonel Marion to go on sick leave.

Sadly, Marion packed his bags and left for his country home to wait for his ankle to heal. He felt useless. He wanted to be back leading his troops. He wondered if his careless action might have endangered his men.

A few weeks later, as Marion sat in his garden reading, a messenger arrived.

"Terrible news, sir! The British have taken Charleston!"

"No!" cried Marion, dropping his book. "It can't be!"

"Yes, sir, I'm afraid it's true," said the messenger breathlessly. "They've taken more than 5,000 Americans prisoner."

"Have they taken the army base?" Marion asked, his heart sinking.

"Yes, sir, everything. You would have been captured, too, if you weren't way out here in the country with a bad ankle. It's the worst disaster of the entire war. I don't see how we can beat the British now."

This news depressed Marion. He could not rest while his friends and fellow soldiers were prisoners. He could not sit idly by while America lost the war.

"My ankle is healed well enough," he told himself one July day. "It's time I got back into the fight. I'm a soldier, a soldier without an army— but I'll find a way around that."

Quickly he called a meeting of farmers in his area.

"I know you men are not soldiers," he told

them. "And I know you have crops to tend and families to feed. But we've got to do something to stop the British. I am putting together a private army, and I'd like you to join it." He paused a minute and glanced around at the men in the room. He could see doubt written on their faces.

"You say it'll be a private army?" asked a farmer named Simon Parsons.

"That's right," said Marion. "If you join, you'll be able to come and go as you please. When it's planting season or harvest time, you can go home. And you don't have to come back until you have your own affairs in order."

"How will you pay us?" Simon asked.

"I won't," Marion admitted. "I can't offer you money. I can only offer you my thanks. And you'll know that you are helping our new country in its hour of need."

"How will we get supplies?" asked another man.

"You'll have to furnish your own," Marion said flatly. "Your own boots, blankets, and guns."

"I'd like to help," said Simon, "but we don't stand a chance against the British. Their army is huge. They'd wipe us out in the first open battle."

"Ah," said Marion, smiling, "you're right; they would. But with my army there won't be any open battles."

"What are you talking about?" asked Simon.

Quietly Marion laid out his plan. He did not intend to confront the British. Instead, he wanted to stage a series of quick hit-and-run attacks.

"The idea," he said, "is to attack the way Indians attack. I've seen the Cherokees do it time and time again. They sneak up to a camp in the middle of the night. They hit it fast and hard ... then disappear into the woods."

The faces of the men in the room grew brighter as Marion talked. They liked his plan. It made sense to them. Most important, they believed it would work.

WITHIN a short time, Marion had assembled his private army. They headed off into the swampy lowlands of South Carolina, searching for British camps. The terrain was a nightmare. Cypress swamps stretched for miles. Rivers crossed and recrossed each other in a giant tangle of rushing water. The dense underbrush grabbed and clawed at anyone who tried to crawl through it.

Marion, however, knew the lowlands well. He had been born and raised on the banks of South Carolina's Cooper River. He led his men through hidden trails in the underbrush to find a British camp. When they reached one, they attacked without warning. Then, as quickly as they had come, they disappeared. Marion led them to hiding places that no British soldier could find.

All that fall, Marion and his men sniped away at the British. One night he led them into Black Mingo Swamp. He wanted to make a surprise raid on a nearby British camp. As he neared the camp, he led his men across a wooden bridge. The sound of the horses' hoofs on the wood gave them away. When they reached the camp, the British were waiting for them.

"Quick!" shouted Marion when he realized his mistake. "Back to the swamp! Retreat! Retreat!"

By moving with lightning speed, he and most of his men escaped death. From then on, Marion never crossed a wooden bridge without first laying down blankets to muffle the sound.

AFTER some weeks, a few bedraggled farmers left to return to their crops and families. But most remained. They had grown to love Marion. He was a calm leader, quiet and thoughtful. He treated all of his men with respect. And he never claimed any special privileges for himself.

"It's another night of potatoes," he told his men one evening as he threw some potatoes on the campfire to bake. "I'm sorry we don't have more to eat, but this will have to do."

Later that night, as they sat eating, Marion noticed that Simon Parsons seemed unusually quiet.

"Something wrong, Simon?" he asked.

"Not really, sir," answered Simon weakly. "I'm just feeling a bit sickly tonight."

Without hesitation, Marion handed his own potato to Simon. "Here," he said. "Take mine. You need your strength."

On another occasion, Marion's blanket caught fire as he slept. By the time he awoke, half the blanket was in flames. He put the fire out, but his only blanket was in tatters. Several men offered to give him their own blankets, but he refused.

"Listen," he declared, "I won't take your blankets. I have no right to be warm when you are cold. I am no better than any one of you. When we're fighting the British, you risk your lives just as surely as I risk mine. So don't treat me as though I'm special, because I'm not."

The men said nothing, but they knew Marion was wrong. He *was* special. His stealth and cunning were driving the British crazy.

BY this time, Marion had become a legend. Every British soldier in South Carolina had heard of him. When the sun disappeared at the end of each day, British soldiers grew jumpy. They knew that at any moment, Francis Marion might attack. They strained their ears for the slightest sound of his approach. Frequently they began firing into the empty darkness around them at false alarms.

Finally, in November 1780, British General Charles Cornwallis took stock of the damage Marion had inflicted. Many British soldiers had been killed in the hit-and-run attacks. He wanted to put a stop to Marion's attacks once and for all. He ordered Colonel Banastre Tarleton to track Francis Marion down.

"You're the best soldier I've got," Cornwallis told Tarleton. "I'm sure you can find this Marion. Your mission is to capture or to kill him."

Tarleton set out. He struggled through the wet swamps. No matter how hard he chased Marion, he could not catch him. Marion always found some shortcut to take or some dense bog in which to hide. At last, Tarleton gave up.

"Come on, men," Tarleton said to his troops, "let's go back. The devil himself could not catch this old fox." From then on, Marion was known to everyone as "Swamp Fox."

As the winter dragged on, the tide of battle began to turn. The British were tired. They were unnerved by Marion's continued attacks. That spring, the Americans recaptured many towns and forts. By September 1781, the American army was in a strong position. And with Marion attacking constantly, the British army became more demoralized than ever.

In October 1781, General Cornwallis surrendered to George Washington at Yorktown, Virginia. The Americans had won their revolution and independence. A good share of the credit belonged to Francis Marion, the one and only "Swamp Fox."

Abigail Adams

A Woman With a Mind of Her Own

Mistress Abigail is different. When Master John was in Philadelphia — meeting with the Continental Congress — she just took over! She was able to run the farm, raise four children, and nurse us when we were ill.

And letters! She was always writing letters. She wrote about freedom, liberty, education — in fact, about everything.

Everyone remembers and talks about the men. But here was a woman who matched them. Let me tell you!

Y OU can't run a farm without slaves!" exclaimed William Smith.

"Perhaps. I just know slavery isn't right," insisted Abigail. William knew it was useless to argue with his sister.

"Just because John Adams is your beau," he said, "you think you're an expert in politics."

Abigail shook her head. "Not so, little brother. I say what I think. John likes that quality in me."

John Adams, a young lawyer, was a frequent

visitor at the Smith's house. He enjoyed talking with Abigail. He admired her independent spirit and outspoken nature. Abigail was different from other women. Other women often just sat quietly and listened, but Abigail liked to join in the conversation and talk about the politics of the day.

As the days and weeks went by, John's admiration grew into love. Abigail and John were married in 1764 and moved to his farm in Braintree, Massachusetts. By 1772, they had a family of four children. Abigail enjoyed her new role as wife and mother. Still, she did not give up her interest in politics. She followed current events in Boston and the rest of Massachusetts.

In the early 1770's, the colonists were moving closer and closer to revolution. Abigail felt very strongly that they had to be free from British control. The colonists had to be able to live their own lives and govern themselves.

But she realized that this meant war. This was not a game. People would die. Families would be separated. Great sacrifices had to be made. In spite of all this, she supported the movement for independence. She wrote:

I would rather die free than live as a British subject. Americans have only two choices—liberty or death.

ON June 17, 1774, her husband left to represent Massachusetts in the Continental Congress in Philadelphia.

"Good-bye, my dearest friend," Abigail whispered.

"Good-bye," John replied.

After one last kiss, he climbed up on the buggy. Abigail watched until it disappeared. Her eyes filled with tears. "Oh, I miss you already," she murmured.

Then her thoughts turned to her four young children. Abigail, the oldest, was only nine years old. The others were seven, four, and two. There were also the family servants to think about. Many of them were quite young and needed attention and guidance. In addition, the Adams's house often was filled with many guests. John's brother visited frequently, as did other relatives.

"How will I manage everything all by myself?" she wondered. "Well, I've been alone before. Surely there's nothing here I can't handle."

In John's absence, Abigail did take charge of the farm. She decided to let certain workers go and hire others. She supervised the breeding of the animals. She even sold the family boat, investing the profits in land. She learned skills she had never needed before.

"Mistress Adams, I admire you so much," said one of Abigail's favorite servant girls. "You run this farm as well as any man could."

Abigail smiled. "Women are as capable as men, my dear," she replied. "All we need is the opportunity to prove it."

Abigail soon had even more opportunity to prove her capability. On April 19, 1775, fighting broke out between British soldiers and colonists. The Revolutionary War had begun. After the battle, young American soldiers stopped at Abigail's farm to eat and rest. Her house by the road became a place where soldiers could always find food and shelter.

ON June 17, 1775, Abigail was awakened at dawn. "Is that thunder I hear?" she wondered. "If it rains now, the hay will be ruined!"

She jumped out of bed and looked out the window. "That's not thunder! It's cannon fire! It sounds so close. What if the British invade Braintree? What will we do?" She forced herself to calm down. "Wait. First find out what is really happening."

The children and servants also awoke. She set them down to breakfast. Then she took the spyglass and her oldest children, Abigail and John Quincy, and went to a nearby hill. She saw British ships in the channel between Charlestown and Boston. They were firing at Bunker Hill. The roar of the cannon, white puffs of smoke, and flashes of fire made an unforgettable impression.

"Is this the war, Mama?" John Quincy asked. "Let me see!"

Abigail said a silent prayer. "Yes, John, this is a momentous day. This is a day you will remember for the rest of your life."

They returned to the house with the news of the battle.

"Should we pack to go, Mistress Adams?" asked the servant girl.

"No, there's no need for us to leave yet," said Abigail firmly. "There's too much to do here. We'll stay and see what happens."

All day people filed down the road in front of their house, fleeing from the British. Relatives and neighbors kept advising Abigail to flee with them. But she refused. She explained her reason in a letter:

> I am not easily frightened. If the men are not able to perform their duty to their country, the enemy will find the women to be a race of Amazons.

Abigail's brother-in-law came to the house with a group of recruits. "We're ready to fight, but we don't have many bullets," he told her. "Have you any pewter you could spare?"

"Certainly," replied Abigail. With that, she took all her pewter spoons and put them in the iron pot over the fire. "As soon as they're melted, I'll fill the molds. You'll have bullets before long!"

Later that day she climbed the hill again to check on the battle. The sky above Charlestown was black with smoke. She sank to her knees. Charlestown was burning. The battle was over. The British had won.

More families fled from Boston. Abigail still refused to leave Braintree. She opened the doors of her house and welcomed dozens of homeless women and children.

Abigail worked very hard cooking, cleaning, and doing laundry for all the people. Unfortunately, an epidemic broke out. The fast-moving disease spread illness and death throughout Braintree. Few families were spared.

The epidemic swept through the Adams's household with deadly results. Abigail nursed her youngest son, several of her servant girls, many of her guests, and herself through terrible days. She watched her mother and her brother-in-law suffer painful deaths.

THROUGHOUT these troubled times, Abigail wrote John hundreds of letters. She sent him valuable information about British troops and ships in the Boston area. She sent news about the farm and the children. Always outspoken, she expressed her feelings on many subjects. Abigail wrote to John about the terrible times:

> They say pain makes us strong. If that is true, then I must be as strong as any person on earth.

Neighbors came to Abigail's house for news about Congress. Since her husband was a delegate, she could inform them about how the new government was developing. Citizens were concerned about the form the new government would take.

Abigail also sent John her own opinion about the new government:

> In the new code of laws, I desire you would remember the ladies, and be more generous and favorable to them than your ancestors. Do not put such unlimited power into the hands of the husbands. If particular care and attention are not paid to the ladies, we will not be bound by any laws in which we have no voice, or representation.

She took care of the farm so well throughout this period that she wrote:

> I hope in time to have the reputation of being as good a farmeress as my partner has of being a good statesman.

She saved the farm from ruin during the long years of war. John wrote her that she was a better farm manager than he was.

There was no school during the war, so she was also responsible for the education of her four children. Abigail condemned the education that was offered to females. She wrote:

> I regret the trifling narrow contracted education of the females in my own country.

She made sure that she gave her daughter the same education she gave her sons.

FINALLY, in 1783, the war was over. The thirteen colonies were free and became a new nation.

Abigail and John's years of forced separation were over. They spent the next five years together in Europe as John represented America's interests. When they returned home, John served under George Washington as the first Vice-President of the United States.

In 1797, John Adams became the second President of the United States. Abigail's intelligence and will made her one of the country's greatest First Ladies. She served as her husband's trusted confidante. They shared many conversations as John Adams charted the course for the new nation. Abigail kept reminding him of the role women could assume. Abigail's legacy paved the way for women to enjoy opportunities about which she herself could only have dreamed.

PHILLIS WHEATLEY
THE FIRST BLACK POET

I remember that night so long ago. It seems like a dream, but it wasn't. A full moon shone overhead. Drumbeats filled the air. Our tribe was celebrating the planting season. Suddenly, guns thundered. Our chief slumped to the ground, motionless. The slavers bound us in irons and marched us to the sea. They led us onto the "Great Winged Bird." Down, we walked, down into the dark, dark belly of the ship—to begin our new lives as slaves.

THE young black girl shivered in the drizzling rain. She stood in shackles on the deck of the slave ship as it waited in Boston Harbor in 1761. Around her stood a hundred other blacks, all of them chained to the boat. The girl's eyes flashed with fear as a group of white men and women came on board. She did not know what awaited her. One white woman approached her and studied her face intently.

"John," called the woman to her husband. "I want this one. She has such a sweet, sensitive face. She will be perfect."

"Fine," replied her husband. "I'll speak to the captain and arrange to buy her."

"Now let's see," the woman said later, as she and her husband led the girl off the ship. "You will need a name ... I know. I will call you Phillis."

The eight-year-old girl did not understand a word of English. She had no idea what the woman was saying. She didn't know that she had just been bought by Mr. Wheatley and given a new name — Phillis Wheatley.

Mr. and Mrs. Wheatley led Phillis to a buggy. Phillis had

never seen such a contraption before, and she was frightened. But Mrs. Wheatley spoke to her in a kind and reassuring voice, and finally Phillis climbed in. She sat very still as the horse pulled away from the docks.

"I know you will be very happy here, Phillis," Mrs. Wheatley said as they moved along.

Phillis did not understand the words, but she liked this woman's soft, gentle voice. She was glad to be off the crowded slave ship.

"Perhaps it will not be so bad here," she thought to herself.

Phillis tried to be cheerful, but she thought of her family and felt sad. She knew they were gone forever. She would never again see the soft face of her mother each night as they watched the African sun drop into the sea. She would never walk through dense African forests with her father and listen to the sounds of birds and wild animals. As thoughts of her family filled her mind, Phillis had to blink back her tears.

They arrived at a beautiful house. Phillis had never seen anything like it. It was so big! And the flower garden in front of it brightened the gray day. A girl of about eighteen greeted them at the door.

"Mary, this is Phillis," Mrs. Wheatley said to her daughter. "Phillis is to be my special slave. I will train her to care for me when I grow old. She will do no heavy labor. Instead, she will perform light housework. After that, she will spend her time with me, learning to speak English. And, if she is able to learn to speak English, I may even teach her to read a little."

"Mother! Do you mean that? You're going to teach a slave to read?"

"Well, why not? Oh, I know that most slaves can't read. But, Mary, look at this girl's face. See how bright her eyes are. There's something about her that seems special. It would be wonderful if she could read the Bible to me when my eyes grow too weak to see clearly."

Mary looked at Phillis carefully. "Well," she said, "I guess it's possible, Mother. You are a very good teacher. And I can help, too."

AS Phillis settled into the Wheatley household, she grew more confident. Everyone treated her with kindness and respect. Thoughts of her family and her homeland in Africa were always with her, but each day the sadness faded a little. Besides, she was busy learning about the challenging new world that surrounded her.

Phillis especially enjoyed the English lessons that Mrs. Wheatley gave her.

"This is exciting," she thought. "It's a whole new way of speaking. So many new words ... and so much to learn ... I just hope Mrs. Wheatley won't get upset with me when I make mistakes."

In fact, Mrs. Wheatley found Phillis's progress amazing.

"Can you believe it?" she said to Mary one day. "Why, Phillis has been here just a few months, and already she's speaking English beautifully."

Mary had to admit that it was astounding. "I wonder what else she could learn?" she said thoughtfully.

"Let's find out!" said Mrs. Wheatley.

During the next years, Mrs. Wheatley and Mary taught Phillis many things. They taught her to read. They taught her Greek mythology and the Latin classics. They also taught her history, geography, and astronomy.

"Phillis, how can you learn these things so quickly?" asked Mary in admiration. "Why, it's taken me years of study to reach this level. And you are already able to do more than I am! You are truly exceptional!"

Phillis thought awhile before she replied. "I don't know—it seems to come easily. I only know that I want to learn as much as I can. The world is so large, so beautiful. Your books tell me about

faraway places and my heart races. I always want to learn more."

Her memories of Africa had grown dim, but new thoughts were filling her mind. She read of great men and women who had overcome hardships. She was inspired. "What can I do?" she thought. "Surely there is a place for me in this great beautiful world."

ABOUT five years later, when Phillis was fourteen years old, Mrs. Wheatley gave her a book of poems written by Alexander Pope. As Phillis read the poems, she became more and more excited.

"These poems are beautiful," she thought. "I think I love poetry most of all."

As Phillis studied Pope's works, a new idea came to her. "I wonder if I could write poems as clever as these?" she asked herself. "It's worth a try." She sat down with a pencil and a piece of paper and began to write a poem. When she finished, she stared at it for a long time.

"I'm not sure it's good enough to show anyone," she thought. She tucked it into a book and left it there for several days. Finally, she gathered her courage and presented it to Mrs. Wheatley.

"Phillis, this is wonderful!" cried Mrs. Wheatley in amazement. "I don't know *anyone* who can write poetry like this! Mr. Wheatley, come see what Phillis has done."

Mr. Wheatley, too, was impressed by the poem. And Mary was delighted with it. From then on, the Wheatleys encouraged Phillis to write more.

Mrs. Wheatley gave Phillis a light for her room. It was a luxury no other slave had.

"This way," said Mrs. Wheatley, "you'll be able to write down a thought or a verse whenever you feel like it, even if it comes to you in the middle of the night."

GRADUALLY, Mrs. Wheatley introduced Phillis to some of her friends. She wanted them to see just how special Phillis was. At first, these women didn't believe that Phillis could read or write. But when they met Phillis, their attitudes changed. They were enchanted by her fine manners and graceful conversation. Later, when they read her poems, they were truly impressed.

"You are able to do what few others, white or black, have the ability to do," Lucy Coldwell told her. "I feel honored to know you."

Phillis enjoyed the attention. But one thing bothered her.

"They say I am their equal," she thought. "They say in some ways I am superior to them. But legally, I am still a slave, without freedom or rights. I will always have to live in the Wheatley household. I will perform household tasks each day at their bidding. I will never travel or see the world." Sorrowfully, she looked around her lovely home and realized it was not enough.

In 1770, at the age of 17, Phillis published her first poem. She wrote it in honor of the Reverend George Whitefield, who died in September of that year. People who read the poem admired it. They felt it was a fitting tribute to a great man.

ALL at once, at the age of 20, Phillis's health began to fail. Mrs. Wheatley became concerned and took Phillis to the doctor. The doctor suggested that sea air might improve her condition. The Wheatleys' son Nathaniel was traveling by ship to England in May of 1773, and the Wheatleys decided to send Phillis with him.

As Phillis stood on the dock of Boston Harbor saying good-bye to the Wheatleys, she thought back to the first time she had seen the harbor. She could still remember the slave ship that had brought her to America. She grew quiet, thinking of that frightening time. Mrs. Wheatley's gentle voice interrupted her thoughts.

"We have a little gift for you in honor of your trip," she said to Phillis. She nudged Mr. Wheatley, and he pulled some papers out of his coat pocket.

"Here," he said, smiling. "Here are your freedom papers."

"What?" cried Phillis.

"That's right," said Mrs. Wheatley. "We have

decided that you should not be a slave any longer. These papers officially make you a free woman."

"Thank you," cried Phillis, embracing them both. "You have been wonderful masters, but I am so happy to be free. You'll never know how much this means to me."

In England, Phillis met many important people. She dazzled them with her grace, charm, and intelligent conversation. While in London, she even published a collection of her poems. It was called *Poems on Various Subjects, Religious and Moral.*

By the time Phillis returned to America four months later, she had become a famous black poet. She stood as a symbol for the strength of the human spirit. She had met with many difficulties in her life. She had been taken from her family and sold as a slave. She had been thrown into a culture that was completely new to her. She was a black female living at a time when neither blacks nor females had equal rights. Yet she had risen above all these things, and had gone on to greatness.

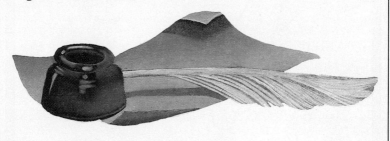

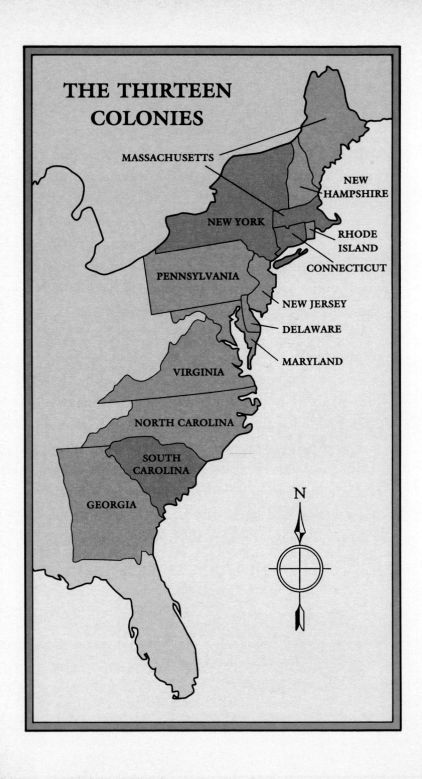

THE THIRTEEN COLONIES

MASSACHUSETTS

NEW HAMPSHIRE

NEW YORK

RHODE ISLAND

CONNECTICUT

PENNSYLVANIA

NEW JERSEY

DELAWARE

MARYLAND

VIRGINIA

NORTH CAROLINA

SOUTH CAROLINA

GEORGIA

N